Sports Stars

MOSES MALONE

Philadelphia's Peerless Center

By Hal Lundgren

 CHILDRENS PRESS ™

CHICAGO

Cover photograph: Raff Frano
Inside photographs courtesy of the following:
Bob Kingsbury, pages 6, 17, and 19; Steve Schwartz,
pages 8, 31, and 40; Barry L. Colla, pages 11 and 22;
Raff Frano, pages 13, 27, 29, 34, 36, and 38; Ira
Golden, pages 15, 33, and 42; Bob Goldman, page 24.

Library of Congress Cataloging in Publication Data

Lundgren, Hal.
  Moses Malone : Philadelphia's peerless center.

  (Sports stars)
  1. Malone, Moses, 1955-   —Juvenile literature.
2. Basketball players—United States—Biography—Juvenile
literature. 3. National Basketball Association—
Juvenile literature. I. Title. II. Series.
GV884.M19L86 1983   796.32'3'0924 [B]   82-19921
ISBN 0-515-04328-5

4 5 6 7 8 9 10 11 12 R 90 89 88 87 86 85

Sports Stars

MOSES MALONE

Philadelphia's Peerless Center

Until Moses Malone came into pro basketball, he was always a big kid.

Moses was 6 feet 2 inches tall when he was 13. As a high school sophomore, he was 6 feet 9 inches. By his senior year at Petersburg (Virginia) High School, Moses had grown another inch. He was 6 feet 10 inches.

Then he did what few high school basketball players are good enough to do. He chose to skip college. He went right into pro basketball.

After high school Moses went into pro basketball, skipping college. He does not think that was a mistake for him.

For most young men, Moses's choice would have been a bad one. College or other training is important when you are 18. Moses didn't think he needed either one.

"I wanted to be a pro basketball player," Moses said. "That's the one, God-given talent I have. I decided that if I wanted to be a pro basketball player, I could have learned as quickly by playing pro basketball as by playing college basketball." So, he chose to turn pro.

Recruiters, those men who wanted Moses to sign to play basketball at their college, were sad. More than 200 of them had written, phoned, or even visited Moses.

"We had five hotels in Petersburg," Moses said. "There was at least one recruiter at each of them all the time. Every time I left my house, I saw one of those guys."

After Moses made his decision to be a pro player, there was no turning back. He was drafted by the Utah Stars of the American Basketball Association (ABA). After that happened the rules would not let him ever play college basketball.

Some men in their teens and 20s try to play pro basketball when they are too young. Most of them are sorry later. They see that they have made a mistake. But it is too late to be a college athlete. That is against the rules after they become pros.

Moses always has been a humble athlete. When Utah drafted him, Moses at first did not believe the news. He was playing in a Petersburg gym. His friends told him he had been chosen.

"I told them they were crazy," Moses said. "When I drove home, I heard it on the radio. I knew it was true."

Moses didn't stay with Utah for a long time. His contract was sold to St. Louis one year later. The ABA did not stay around long either. It went out of business. But Moses lasted a long time. He played for four pro teams in the National Basketball Association (NBA). Then he was traded to Houston in October, 1976. It was there he became a star.

Moses has the ball on a rebound and will pass out to start a fast break.

Moses's story has a happy ending. He was better off in the pros. So, after a year or two in Houston, people began saying he was the best offensive rebounder in the history of basketball.

It was a wonderful compliment. Offensive rebounding means grabbing rebounds from your team's basket—the basket your team is shooting at. Defensive rebounding is easier because you are closer to the basket on defense.

Moses's secret, he said, is "to watch the flight of the ball. I see where the ball is going to bounce. I try to get to that position as fast as I can."

He knows what will happen to most missed shots.

"Most of the really good shooters will miss long," he explained. "Especially the ones who shoot those soft, arching floaters. They sort of slide up there. You've got to know if a player shoots a flat shot or shoots with an arch."

Now that his life is going well, would Moses make the decision to skip college today?

"I'd do it again if I were in the same situation," he said. "I can't say it'd be the right thing for everybody. But it was in my case."

Malone's success was no easy thing. Even before he was born there wasn't much chance he'd be an NBA center, much less a star. His father was only 5 feet 6 inches tall. His mother was 5 feet 2 inches. When Moses signed his first pro contract, one of the first things he did was buy his mother, Mary, a new home. Not a bad thank-you present.

"I didn't notice it being rough when I was a kid," he recalls. "I had a lot of friends.

"I became very close to my mother. I had no brothers or sisters. She had to be my brother, my sister, and my father, too. She became all those to me.

"I think I'm a lucky person to have grown up around someone like her."

A center as great as Moses usually plays for only one or two teams. Before he became a star, Malone played for Utah, St. Louis, Portland, and Buffalo. St. Louis went out of business when the ABA folded. The other three teams gave up on Moses. Utah sold Moses to St. Louis. Both Portland and Buffalo traded him. But Moses said he wasn't hurt by all his moving around.

"It didn't bother me," he said. "I knew I could play the game. I knew it was just a matter of getting on the right team.

"I didn't think any of the trades were a knock at me. I was confident I would wind up on a team that wanted me. I didn't worry. I knew the moving around would stop."

Moses made it, in part, on his talent. But hard work kept him going when other players would have lost heart.

Moses worked on shooting, which every player loves to do. He also worked on being at the right place on the court at the right time. Not every player likes to work at that. It is boring. It's much less fun than shooting.

Moses is about to release a jump shot.

Some experts say Moses's talent and his work habits have made him the most important player in pro basketball. The men who write about pro basketball for America's newspapers certainly think he is. They voted him the Most Valuable Player Award for the whole league in 1982. He also won the award in 1979.

There is a strange thing about Moses. In a land of giants, he is one of the shorter men. Still 6 feet 10 inches, he plays the center position against taller men in almost every game.

Kareem Abdul-Jabbar of Los Angeles is at least 7 feet 2 inches. Some men who play against Abdul-Jabbar claim he really is 7 feet 4 inches.

Moses does not have hands as big as most basketball players his size.

That would make him six inches taller than Moses. Moses also does not have the bulging muscles of a Darryl Dawkins or a Bob Lanier.

Even when Moses goes up against a player no taller than himself, there is a big problem. None of the other NBA giants have it. Moses has tiny hands. Julius Erving, the famous Dr. J, is six inches shorter than Moses. Yet Erving's hands are larger than Moses's.

When Moses was taller than his opponents in high school, those hands were no problem.

"By the time I was a sophomore, I could go up and get the rebound with one hand. Then I'd pass with the same hand without ever touching it with my left hand," Moses said.

The problems came later in life.

Moses's small hands give him problems when opposing pro players slap at the ball. Large, strong hands can grip a ball so firmly that a player on the other team cannot swat it loose.

Moses used to make things even harder for himself. He tried to dribble with opponents next to him. They tried to take the ball away when he dribbled. They often succeeded.

That's where Moses's hard work helped him solve a problem. He practiced what to do instead of dribbling. He practiced holding the ball, shooting the ball, and passing it to a teammate. He kept on practicing. Now nobody sees Moses losing the ball on a dribble. His hard work paid off again.

"I have never, ever gone around claiming I was the greatest player in the league," Moses once said. "But I have always thought I was one of the hardest workers."

Moses also claims he is not among the best 10 players in the game. This may be his way of teasing.

Moses gets to the right place at the right time to get a rebound.

"I'm probably about 12th," said Moses.

When he was asked who is better, he could name no names. But he replied, "Everybody seven feet tall."

Moses's shooting would not have caught everybody's eye as a young player. He scored his points close to the basket. When he turned pro, the other big men did not always let him get close enough to the basket to score. Moses worked on shooting from farther away. Now he is a good shooter from 15 to 18 feet from the basket. People who say Moses Malone is only a good rebounder are wrong. They forget that in both 1981 and 1982 he finished second in the NBA in scoring.

Moses has never been noisy when he does something well. He tried to say the right things about his teammates and his opponents. He made the mistake of saying the wrong thing only once in recent years. He actually popped off.

The Rockets were playing in Boston. It was a seven-game series for the 1981 NBA Championship. Moses said, "Me and four guys from Petersburg could beat the Celtics."

The Celtics were insulted. Several of them were angry. They beat Houston for the championship. Moses was sad. He probably never again will say anything bad about another team.

Often more than one man covers Moses.

Moses seldom has anything to gripe about. Two and three opponents often try to stop him from scoring. They grab and bump him, but are not always called for fouling him. His coach in Houston, Del Harris, remembered seeing Moses fight off several men.

"Robert Parish plays for the Boston Celtics," Harris said when someone claimed Parish should have been voted most valuable player. "Parish sees mostly one-on-one defenses.

"On the other hand, the scouting report on us says that if you double- or triple-cover Moses, you have a better than average chance of beating our team. As a result, Moses is always ganged up on. But night after night he goes out

In 1982 Moses was traded to the Philadelphia 76ers.

there. And he is able to come through with the kind of All-Star performances that got us all the way to the finals in 1981."

The coach was right. Moses's teammates were not as good as Parish's teammates in Boston or Abdul-Jabbar's teammates in Los Angeles. It was up to Moses to pick up his team. And he did. He missed only one of Houston's 82 games in the 1982 season.

In the late summer of 1982 Moses was traded to the Philadelphia 76ers. It will be easier for Moses to play in Philadelphia. They have better players than Houston did.

"I don't want to have to be the leading scorer every night," he said.

Moses is an easy man to be around.

"It would be real nice to get into a situation where I could play 35 to 38 minutes a night. Then have a good backup center to come in and let me rest for 10 or 12 minutes. I think I could play for another seven years doing that.

"I can play a lot of minutes. My body can handle it. I can set my mind to play the full game if I have to."

That's just like Moses. Cooperative. Unlike some superstars who keep people waiting, Moses is easy to be around. Teammates say he was always on time when the Rockets practiced, met, or went to the airport for a trip.

Of course, he's early when a game is to be played.

"There never is an excuse for not being ready to play," he said. "If they wake you at 4 o'clock in the morning and tell you to go and play a game, you ought to be ready to go to work."

Moses's work shows up in all those rebounds he grabs. He led the league for the Rockets. His 19 offensive rebounds in one game and 587 in one season are NBA records. No wonder he is called the greatest rebounder in pro basketball history.

Moses played very well for the Philadelphia 76ers. The Sixers won the NBA by beating the Lakers in the first four games. Because of his playing, Moses was named Most Valuable Player.

Many people call Moses the greatest rebounder in pro basketball history.

CHRONOLOGY

1955—Moses Malone is born on March 25 in Petersburg, Virginia.

1968—At age 13, Moses shows signs of being a great basketball player. He is 6 feet 2 inches tall

1974—Moses graduates from Petersburg High after leading his team to the state championship. One of its wins in the state tournament is by a score of 95 to 43.

1974—The Utah Stars draft Moses out of high school. He signs to play with the American Basketball Association team on August 24.

1975—Utah sells Moses to St. Louis on December 3.

1976—When the ABA goes out of business, Portland of the National Basketball Association signs Moses on August 5.

1976—Portland chooses to keep Bill Walton, not Moses Malone, as its center. Moses is traded to Buffalo October 18. Walton soon retires because of injuries.

1976—Houston, which had been admiring Moses all along, trades two first-round draft choices and some money to Buffalo for Moses on October 25.

1979—After setting a league record with 587 offensive rebounds, Moses is honored in June as the NBA's Most Valuable Player.

1981—Though Houston's team is not one of the best, it has Moses. Moses leads the Rockets to the NBA finals, where Boston wins the series, four games to two.

1982—Moses scores 53 points against San Diego on February 2. It is his career high.

1982—On June 16, Moses is honored for the second time as the league's Most Valuable Player.
  —On September 15 Moses is traded to Philadelpl a. His pay will be $13 million for the next six years.

1983—Moses is named the NBA's Most Valuable Player and Philadelphia sweeps over the Lakers to win the NBA.

1984—Moses is the top rebounder in the NBA.

ABOUT THE AUTHOR

Hal Lundgren has covered many sports since joining the *Houston Chronicle* sports staff in 1968. He has been a close observer of Moses Malone since he joined the Rockets in 1976.

Mr. Lundgren is married and has two sons. He is president of the Houston Sportswriters and Sportscasters Association. He is also a member of the Pro Football Hall of Fame selection committee. His other interests include participating in a city basketball league, playing trumpet with a brass ensemble, serving as commissioner of a youth baseball league, and following the stock market.

Mr. Lundgren has written two other books for Childrens Press in the Sports Stars series; *Earl Campbell: The Texas Tornado* and *Calvin Murphy: The Giant Slayer.*